Writing and Publishing a Book (Pocket Size)

Writing and Publishing a Book (Pocket Size)

SECRETS OF A CHRISTIAN AUTHOR

Bill Vincent

RWG Publishing

CONTENTS

RWG Publishing

PO Box 596

Litchfield, IL 62056

https://rwgpublishing.com/

Published in the United States of America

1

Writing and Publishing a Book

Publishing a manuscript is what we're going to talk about. I would like to begin with a question "why should you write" because a lot of people have a desire to do things, but they can't justify why and some people may not be ready to write because they can't answer the first question, and why should anybody even want to read what you write. So, that's an important question, to begin with. Do you have a purpose for what you desire to do, so here are some questions? And some answers that we can talk about why you should write because first of all, the world is ruled by dead men. How can dead men rule the world? Very simple because dead men left their ideas on paper, and that's what writing does? When you write, you are leaving a legacy. It gives you the power, the ability to leave your thoughts beyond your grave; that's because ideas outlive men. All of us have great ideas. Some are still cultivating and developing those ideas, but those ideas are essential, and I think the first thing you might need to get over is that you do have ideas that are worth reading. I think the average person might feel like, what do I have to say to the world, who wants to read what I have to write? And that barrier can stop you from writing. You almost assume that other people are opposed to writing, but not you. So, you enjoy reading other people's ideas, and never thinking that perhaps you may have something worth reading. So, those issues we want to reset, we want to sell them.

Another point when and why should you write because your ideas should live beyond your generation. Nothing is as powerful as a book, no matter how much they develop electronic technology. The book will remain supreme, they now have e-books that you can buy, but there are still books, and somebody's going to write that manuscript to download into that e-book. So, writing is always permanent. It'll be forever. No matter how you use electronic media, someone has to write the content so that the book will live forever. Also, books are so important that God used one himself. And God preserved his ideas for humanity, not on a C.D, not on tape, and not on a DVD. He preserved his ideas in a book, so if God uses books to preserve divine knowledge, how much more should we use the instrument and the medium of a book to preserve our ideas to outlive our generation.

When you go to college, and you pay money to study, you pay money to read books. A college education is you not being disciplined enough to read books by yourself. So, you pay someone to make you go to the library and read, and that is called a college the power of ideas. You go to a college to get ideas, and then they certify you when you get a certain amount of ideas. It's called a certificate or a diploma. So, books are so vital that you pay an institution to make you read them. And what are in those books' ideas, so why should you write? Well, because you want to document your ideas because documented ideas gain credibility. Now, what do I mean by that? If you speak ideas as a public speaker, whether you are a motivational speaker or a teacher in a classroom, or a preacher in a pulpit or a politician, those ideas will normally die as soon as you finish talking, and they would only be credible to the point of people's knowledge of you. In other words, based on what they know about you, that will determine how much credibility they will give to the ideas coming from your mouth, but the minute you write your ideas on paper, something happens to them. There is a tendency in humanity to believe anything that is written, even though it may not be true. Once you document it, it receives credibility. This is why you can document foolishness, and people will buy it. Because once you write it, it gains credibility. That's why you should write. Writing will automatically give credibility to your ideas.

Why should you write? Because writing gives you life. It also brings life to readers. Beyond on your grave, a book will outlive you all the time because the book freezes your experience; it makes you eternal. It makes you speak beyond your grave. Writing allows you to multiply and expand your influence; you might be able to speak to one audience that could be ten to thousands, but that's it. The world has billions of people. When you write a book, your ideas can go beyond you and enter countries you'd never thought possible that you've never visited, you will enter people's homes that you can never get into legally, you will enter universities and schools and colleges and children's lives and young people's lives who will never invite you in, but they'll invite your book. So, your book and your writing will give you influence. It expands your capacity to impact people. And this is why writing is important.

Another reason why you should write is you should be qualified. Now, what qualifies you to write first is that you must have experience. People don't want you to tell them other people's ideas because they can go to those people and get them themselves. They want to hear your experience, all of us have experience with life and with the truth. And so, you need to begin to think about it and gather and begin to document your experience with life.

Second qualification, you must have a clear idea. Many times, people ask me what's the first step in writing a book. And my answer is...do you have an idea?. Don't use the word idea. I'm talking about a big idea that is so important to you. That you believe everyone else should know about that idea. Maybe as an experience, you had an understanding that you got about life, an experience that you had in life that became so important to you that you want to share with other people. That's what I call the big idea. You know every excellent book only has one idea in it. And you build the whole book around that idea, every book on my table. Then the lobby has one idea in it. And everything is built around that idea. You keep building around it so that people walk away from that book with one idea, your one message. So, the question is, do you have a clear message, a clear idea that you can grow and document.

The third thing is the qualifications for writing a book is you must test and prove the idea if it works for you. If this idea, when impacted would change your entire experience and transform your life. You have the beginnings of a qualification to write. Put your thoughts in writing. Sometimes, I've seen people take my books, read them, and then collect information from my book and write a book from my information. That's not a clear idea;

I've tested these ideas myself, so they are mine in the book I've proven that they work. You need to go and get your proof. So, you can read. And by the way, if you're going to be a writer, you gonna be a reader. You have to read a lot of books. There's nothing new under the sun. What is there are combinations of all things? So, a writer never writes anything new. They write it from a new perspective — a new means their experience with it. So, if you're going to be a writer, then you have to be a reader. You have to have had an experience with what you want to write. Now, there are different types of books. So, I want to be cautious here. For example, if you're writing poetry, it may be exquisite experiences that you have in life that you capture and in prose, and you want to write a poet poetry book. That's different writing, or if you're going to write a journal from your experience and maybe traveling or when ministry or whatever you do. That's different writing you are recording your experience, and you can put it in a book, and people can enjoy that, or you may want to write a fiction book. It's a different kind of book, but it still needs to have an idea in it, for example, Star Wars© is a fiction series of books and if you study Star

Wars© it's really about one idea, and everything is built around the idea and they've written many different volumes of that, which became movies that made billions of dollars, but they still have an idea in those books. But that writing is not necessarily from experience; it's from a creative bent of fiction where you have a creative mind to capture ideas and put them in a fictional form. I believe that most people that will read this have a different type of writing, which is writing that may be inspirational, educational, teaching, training, and experiential.

I assume you are thinking about those manuscripts, and that's what we're going to talk about. Next qualification to write, ask yourself this question. Is the idea helpful to the greater market? In other words, you shouldn't write because everybody else is writing. You should write because you experienced an idea, or you experienced some truth or some encounter with life that you believe other people could also experience with you. So, you want to share that idea. You want to distribute it. You want to multiply it; then, you're qualified to write if you had a good experience in a roach; you know women would be interested in that. Can a greater market consume this, and it can be beneficial to them, but if the answer is No, then you haven't gotten an idea yet to write because I've seen some books that shouldn't be on the shelf. One of the worst places to find good materials is in a Christian bookstore because people got so many shallow experiences in these books. They're just like duplications of what you know from shallow experiences, and there's no real deep contribution to a person's life. Some folks want to see their pitch on the back of a book. Or their name on it. There's no content, and there's no, I don't. I don't sit on a sit when I write a book. I have never done that. All of the books I've written are from an experience that produced a change in me that impacted my life and transformed my perspective of life. And it's readjusted my life, and it was so real to me every time I said this would help people, and it becomes the idea that I build the manuscript around. Are you qualified to write? You must research your idea; once you capture something that you think the world should know about. Maybe a perspective of something then you need to begin to research on that subject as well because your experience with it is not enough, you need to read more. That's why you read a broader perspective of it. Get other people's views on it. You want to get more depth, so you can have even a richer understanding of what you experienced. A good book would have references and quotes from other people who can further enhance your idea. This is where people get lazy and want to research again. This is why you have to read to be a writer. If you don't like to read, you won't be a successful writer. You have to read other people's works. You have to read far and wide and broad, and you must be able to do proper research. Now, the third question is ... what do you write?

Well, here are some thoughts. This is very important. Always write your passion, you know if you are trying to write something that you are not passionate about, you will find it almost impossible to finish that manuscript. You will be quickly paralyzed by procrastination because there's no passion or interest in you. In essence, you shouldn't just sit down and say OK I want to write a book where and you shoot, but there's no motivation for the idea. Good writers never sit down and say, Let me see what I want to write about. Good authors never do that. Good authors are almost driven to let something out of them. That's what makes it a good book. I normally tell people. Look, if you are a public speaker, and your ideas are what you communicate to the public, and this could be a motivational speaker; it could be a coach. You can be a pastor, a preacher, a priest, or someone who is always speaking their ideas to people. Well, you have to find out what message is your passion. In essence, I always asked people who want to be an author, what is your word to the world, and everybody has a word to the world? The world usually doesn't allow you to develop that word, but everyone has something to say to the world. In other words, I am convinced that in every human, there is, at least, one book and that book is a bestselling book. The problem is we try to mimic other people, try to write what other people write and never find our passion. So, write your passion past the standard forsaken. Yeah, I'll ask you a question. I want you to think in five seconds and answer me. What is your word to the world? What do you preach, that is you? And you always come back to it. What is it? What is it like? Life to the fullest.

See now what he is telling me is that no matter what, you asked him to speak on. He's going to end up on life to the fullest. That's how you know what your word is. This speaks on money, money to make up like that for another. You keep coming back to your work. That's your passion, so your first book should be your passion. Because your passion is believable, and then you pick that book up. They should feel the passion in your manuscript because it's coming out of your very spirit. You know if you've got to make up things to write, you're not writing your passion.

So you're going to write a book for the first time, don't go to the bookstores and look at it with titles and then choose a title that you want to write on because I know it looks nice. What is your passion? First, it's easier to write it. You are more motivated to write it. It's natural to write it. You will be excited when you write it, and it begins to explode like a river. Breaking the banks when it starts coming up because it's a passion, the second thing you should write about is your experience, and nothing is easy to talk about than what you experienced. So, write about your experience with whatever you can talk about the best. Write about it, whatever makes you feel real. Write that, and your experience of it makes you feel real.

I have never written a book because I decided it's a good idea. You know one of the reasons why the publishing companies love me, and I say this respectfully because I have about four publishing companies that compete for me and all trying to get me, even though I own a publishing company. Do you know why? Because I'm a very weird author, some of the books I've written became a best-selling book, authors don't do that, and people ask me how did you do that. How did you, is it possible for you to have your 50 books out of 50 best-selling books? That's impossible. It's because I don't just sit down and read. I write my experience and my passion, I write what has happened on the point of explosion in my life, something that deeply moved me, that changed me. So, it always comes out with that passion, and people will buy your passion, you know Rick Warren, for example, he wrote this book on the Purpose Driven Life that was from a series that he taught, and he got his ideas from some people. I won't tell you who they are now. But it became his passion. He caught something from the information and began to teach it to his church, and it lasted almost a year. And it became his passion not as difficult to follow up a successful book just because you were successful with a book because you have got to find another passion. So, because you are successful in one book doesn't mean you have got to make another book. People are still looking for the passion that's why you'll find good authors with a bestselling book one year, and then you don't hear about them for three-four years, and then they bring books out, but they keep falling flat because they haven't again found a passion on what to write.

Write your testimony; testimony is things that you tested again because whatever your testimony in your life is real to you so you can write on it easily. Number four, write your revelation. And again, this is not a scary word. Revelation means something came on in your life like a light boom, and you understand it, and I mean it explodes in you.

What I'm asking for is to give me your passion because you will die. We will lose it. Document your passion, write your revelation. That's what I do, and another thing is to write your obligation. Here's a weird one. If you want to be a good writer, write what you believe, you are obligated to leave the world. Do you feel a responsibility to leave?

Would life have taught you to the next generation that's writing your obligation? You must feel obligated to get this on paper before you die. That's what you should write, write your obligation.

Another thing is writing your conviction, don't write other people's convictions because theirs are not yours. You need to write what you discovered yourself. You must write what happened to you, in which you genuinely believe what you have been convinced. Let that be the source of your manuscript because people will pick that. Write the words; people will read your convictions. They're supposed to feel the conviction, and every line you write should lead them to your conviction that's what you wrote. A good question is when do you write? When should I start writing the first answer is essential, right? Where. There is a demand for it. For example, I have been speaking on the Jezebel Spirit for over the years, and I've been speaking on Prophetic over 20 years, I've been speaking on the Presence of God for the years. I wrote one of my first books, "The Secret Place of God's Power." A well-known publisher picked it up and sold 100,000 copies.

The problem was that I only received $8000.00

in royalty. This is what birthed RWG Publishing, and my real passion for writing exploded. This was all written from sermons. They took the recordings of my words preached. Then they organize it into chapters. The manuscript of me writing a single word was what I wrote with my tongue. They documented my tone, and I said that in my home with this manuscript for the first time in my life with my name on it, and he said go through it to see whatever you want to take out, change or add, review and revise is totally up to you. And I went through the whole thing, and I did my addiction, my adjustments and added some things, and I sent it back to them. They added those things and sent it back to me, and after three or four, they did those exchanges to clean everything up, they said okay we're ready to print, and they publish the book. My point is there was a demand before there was a book. You know if you decide to write a book, no one may even want to read it. You need to talk about your ideas to test them on people. So, you can test the interests of the market for your ideas. There are millions of books on the shelves that are not being sold.

So, the demand from people shows they are not

obligated to buy your book because you published it. You have to make sure that there's a demand for your idea, so you have to test your idea, timing is vital for releasing a book, the environment is essential. Important for dealing with the environment, many books are coming out now on how to buy a house in downtime, more books will sell on know how to make your money grow in tough times, and you look at the bookshelves, and all books coming out because of the environment, so you don't just write a book because you have an idea, make sure that there's a demand for it. When you are competent in your idea, then you should write a book. Don't write a book because you've got a few thoughts about it. You have to be competent, which means you have to know this subject matter through and through. It is driven passionately into your bone. It's in your blood. You've done research, you believe it. You are convinced about you, convicted about it. This thing is possessing you. You are competent in your idea. You have done your homework. You know this idea, and you know your enemy.

Now, another thing is when should you write when you have tested your idea before. When should you write when you have proven that your idea works, when should you write? Usually, people write because they've been trying something for a long time. They've been proving that it works on other people. You need to make sure that what you want to leave in print is proven. Why should you write when the market needs your idea? Some of you right now need to write because of what you've been experiencing in your job, your work, your studies, and your experience, what the world needs right now is a good time to write for some people depending on what you've been competent in by the way I'm not a normal man. So, you know I'm a strange guy. Most people in life are good at one thing. My problem is I am good at a lot of things, and this is very rare. And I've been told that by publishers, they said look, we have no author who can write on ten subjects, and they are also bestsellers. They said no one does that, you know.

I'm not boxed in, so my books read books. What I mean is there are many types of books in me. They can go to a Christian bookstore and be in Wal-Mart and be in books a million, and be in all the secondhand books at the same time because they are multi-market books. The ideas are muddy.

Not everybody can do that. So, you need to check your diversity and your ability to expand your market when should you write. Write when a market is demanding your idea; you may be professional in different areas. You should think about putting your ideas on paper if they relate to the present conditions.

How do you write is the question, but first, you should conceive the idea to become like a pregnant woman, your idea should be deeply rooted in you? This idea I can see it. It's clever. I know what it is, what it means. You can see this idea, and sometimes, it takes a long time to conceive an idea. You may have to talk about it for years, and all of a sudden, one day, you realize I've got something here. People are using it. They're believing it is helping people. Maybe I need to crystallize this and freeze it documented, so you've got to begin with a conceived idea. Then the second stage of a book is conceptual content. You must conceptualize the content that would make that idea palatable.

In other words, you may have one clear idea, but now, you have to develop the content that you see in that book to support that idea. That has to be conceptual already, and that leads you to the third level of writing, and that is you can write an outline. Outlines are essential because they put the entire book on one sheet of paper, and you can see all your ideas laid out. Conceptual writing is just like what you learned in school. That's the writing part. You know that they say write an essay, and your teachers taught you to foresee or write an outline. You know you got to write in sequins and put support arguments and all that is important in writing. That's why writing an outline is critical, an outline can be simple lines or can be paragraphs, depending on how much you want to develop it. An outline is essential because it is so valuable that you can set an outline to a publisher and get a contract fantastically, they will sign a contract with you with just an outline. If your outline is properly done, solid idea is sequential, content good, and research documentation to back it up. They will literally call you and say, look, we want to publish this book for you, and we'll pay you. So, don't take the outline lightly, on my computer, I have outlines of about 20 books that I haven't written yet, and that's why the publishers visit me, they come fishing. And I know I'm very conscious I hold them back, I keep those things secret until

I'm ready to consider contractual discussions, your outline is critical. When you tell me you want write a book, I will ask you for the main idea and an outline, you send out to me I will write, look at it, and I tell you, you don't have a book here because the outline tells me whether you have a conceptual view of your idea and you've got the content already listed on paper that will back up your idea, support your arguments.

An outline is powerful, after the outline, then you research. Research means that you begin to read other authors, go on the Internet get information, you can check to know definitions of words. All this is the research; you want to research, gather information, validate your ideas so that you will not have a book that is not solidly referenced. Some people write books that shouldn't be on shelves because there's no research on 80 percent of the books in the Christian bookshops. I will never read. Why? Because we're lazy people who write their experiences without references, without research, you've got to do research. And then, after you have done your research, you compose antidotes and examples. These are important when you're writing a book. You don't just write books.

I've read some manuscripts that are so boring. I have read books that have one sentence and four scriptures. So, this is not a book. This is the bible reference that you are creating and calling it a book. Remember now, and you are writing because you got an idea that you are passionate about. You need to have some examples of other ideas.

So, you want to have examples of descriptions, and you want to have antidotes, little stories to help bring your idea home now. What's wonderful today is you can go on the Internet and get a million stories free. Did you know that as a matter of fact, anything went right on? So, you were to write on dogs, type in dogs and put dog stories on Google, you'd have a thousand dog stories you can use in your book there's no excuse, but that's called research that takes time. And you are so quick to get your book out; you don't have time, so few people buy your book. Another great key is, record your content. That means start writing your content. You can start with the introduction, and you can move on down slow; you can write by hand if you can't type, of course. Computers are a great tool because you get to keep things and adjust them and change them. You start recording your ideas not writing for those of your public speakers. You have an advantage if you're a public speaker; from this day forward, if you want to become an author, you should record everything you speak on, every time you get it. Even if you go to speak on an event somewhere, tell them you want to record it, and you want a copy, I do it every time. Why? Because that content could be a chapter in your book. You did your research; you prepared yourself to speak. You did all of your planning for speaking. You got the examples of your stories already; it's in the speech. So now, you use that and transcribe it. That's what publishers do. They would transcribe your recorded message about why you wrote with your tone, so be conscious all the time that I can write books from a series. And if you teach in series, it's easier for publishers to work with you; I teach in series because I don't preach sermons; I teach principles. So, the Bible is a book of laws, so it's easier for publishers to work with me.

Another Key, write the content, and another is creating a manuscript. Now a manuscript is almost like a finished book, and that's when you begin to see the formal formation of your ideas take shape. You begin to have a flow in this material. It moves successively toward a climax, and you begin to put together your thoughts in order of priority and communication of building support for your idea, a manuscript is almost a complete, book publishers love manuscripts, they represent a lot of money. To the next, review your manuscript content grammar, spelling, you know all kinds of little things now, by the way, you know most of us anagram, are grammar teachers and English teachers, so you need help with this. You're a good editor, get people who understand all that stuff you don't need to be a good grammar writer, to be a good writer, your ideas are more critical in your spelling. Let somebody else pay someone else to spell for you; it's your ideas that sell, not the quality of your writing. That way, writing quality should be good because your grammar is not essential; what's important is that your idea is extra. So, don't sit down trying to spell every word correctly and trying to find ways to better it, you're wasting your time. Your idea is important, and the publishing company provides people to check your grammar, your job is to get your idea in that manuscript, they will clean it up. And miss out on that. That's what you paid him for, all that is their work.

Another key is really seeking endorsements for your manuscript, and endorsement is essential, and a foreword is essential too because again, what you want is to have credibility, especially if you are a new author or an unknown author. You want to have the credibility of someone who is known in the marketplace. So, you seek endorsements. You also can get endorsement from people who are not necessarily authors but who are also well known, perhaps in a specific field. For example, if you're writing a book on economics, you may want to find someone who is well known in economics to endorse the book. You write something, then maybe in marriage, you got to find somebody who is a very famous marriage counselor, not just in the book because those endorsements give credibility every week. I receive, at least, two manuscripts requesting my endorsement or my foreword. Why? Because I'm well-known in the market, and people know that if the content is good and I put my name on it, then they can write my name through the market as it does. You know Michael Jordan gets paid to endorse Nike. You know Tiger Woods. The same thing, Nike then takes the name of the product to the market, so if you have a book and you think it's a good idea, the content is good, and you believe that you want to have opportunities to share this with the world, then you want to seek good endorsements or good people to foreword your product.

Another Key, submit your manuscript. This is important. That means you got to make many copies of it because if you are entering the market as an author, it's a crowded market. Today, you may be able to send it by email as well. The average publisher today receives about 40000 manuscripts a year, you are just one of them on the desks of the mandate of the publisher, wow that's about 4000 manuscripts a month. So, you better, be good. This is why you can have a good manuscript and still not be published because of the time factor, and the competition is high, and everyone's trying to get in the market. And lately, everybody thinks they can write. So, it makes it even worse. Therefore, it does become 80000, and consequently, you have to be good for a publisher to stop and look at your work. You've got to be good. There's got to be something about you that makes them stop all. The other secret is you need someone successful with them to recommend you, any way to leave the pack, so don't think that because you send your manuscript to 10 publishers, you don't get one of them. You're competing with about an average of 40000 manuscripts, each one of those publishing companies gets good contents. I'm convinced it's good enough because my name you know got a particular reputation, I got to protect my name as well. I can't send them junk, so if I tell you to go back and start again, don't be insulted because you embarrass me if I send them junk; they won't wonder about me because they know the standard they're looking for. I know the quality they're looking for, but if I recommend your project to them, my recommendation makes them take it out of the pack and put it on the chief editor's desk because they know me and many others.

You can tell authors who are well known, look, can you submit this for a recommendation with me please, and they can do that, but you've got to submit your mind if you're my new script to the publishers and hope, pray or know someone who knows someone, it's vital when you complete your manuscript. I'm seriously going to pray because the Holy Spirit can speak to a publisher to pull yours out of the pack, I've seen this happen to people. And the publisher would say I don't know why I pulled this out, and then the book becomes a multi-million-dollar bestseller. Because somebody with a brain had a prior manuscript through the system, don't forget God, you can open doors no man can shut. Shut those no man can open. I would give you the process of writing a book.

Now, I'm talking about publishing, now official writing. How do you publish it? First, accept your status as a writer. What that means is look if you are an unknown author say to yourself, I am an unknown author. Accept that no one knows you. Now, you may have a good idea. Good content. A powerful message. The world could be assisted by it, but no one knows you. So, accept it. I am an unknown author who accepts that then we leave you to identify the appropriate publishing company. What do I mean by that? If you are an author just starting, you don't want to send your manuscript to the New York Times, or you know to Portman publishing company in New York. Don't waste your step as you may need to start with a small publishing company, one may be in your neighborhood, or one may be just across the channel. Maybe one that you know also growing and then looking for authors to test themselves with not always knowing where you are in the system and don't lift your expectations so high that you depress yourself when they tell you no.

The other thing is that the appropriate Publishing Company also means your subject matter. If you're writing on love, you don't want to sell the publishing company that you know deals with something else. They will ignore your manuscript. So, the publishing company also will have to be identified. What kind of company is this? What kind of products do they produce? Is that appropriate for what I'm writing on because that helps you get in, is this clear? Some companies publish sportsbooks, but if you want to write on clothing styles, then look at your book. So, you get to what publishing company is this if you have a second a publishing company, and you got this religious book. They may say look, send it to someone else, so you don't think you are going to be accepted by any publishing company because you send something that they might not even open the package. Thirdly, submit the manuscript to many publishers. And your submission can be your recommended publisher if this does not fit your company.

Let's see what they say about this, so you got to send it out. It's just like publishing records music, you know if it is the music industry and you want to publish music, you have to send that C.D. to all kinds of music houses, and one of them might bite. And usually, when you send a manuscript to a publishing company, you want to send a hard copy because you don't know them that well enough to send in a manuscript by email, so you send a hard copy, and they open the box. Take two seconds, look at it, and they don't stop. Let me look at this and then they call you again if you know somebody who knows somebody. It may help with that process. You could tell a publishing company as an author give me a phone call. Look, I'm sending you a publishing manuscript. I want you to take a look at it; this person is a good friend of mine. I think he's got good content and you can send it by e-mail because there's a relationship you're sending it through. Now some publishing companies will tell you. Send me an E-manuscript. You go on the Internet, and there are a million publishing companies out there. They'll let you know if they would receive e-manuscripts, of course, you're taking a chance, but they would make you send it.

I imagine that's out there for the whole world. So, let's say half a million people send a manuscript the same day by email; you're lost right. So even though that's accessible, it may not be the best process. You want to be as close and distinctive as possible, and a hard copy will give you a little more distinction. Then accept and expect rigid rejection, don't expect because you worked so hard on your work that someone is suited as you are. They might even look at it. So, I don't feel you know that you're not good when rejected but know that you are competing with forty thousand people, so you keep trying.

You could then try considering self-publishing, self-publishing is where you decide. No one wants to publish my work, and I will publish it myself. And many companies would be glad to publish your work. You can get it published online right in your house. You can send your manuscript to a company and send your payment. They'll finish all the work for you. They'll do everything; they'll do the editing, they'll do the pagination, they'll do everything for you and send you back a manuscript, you pay them. And then there's if you pay the money and they send you a box of books with your name on the picture and everything else you can do that self-publishing, be willing to pay for publishing if they want to publish a book. Some of these can cost ten thousand dollars. I don't want a published book anymore, would be my answer to that. So, make sure you can manage and budget for publishing because publishing can be costly. A good publishing company would not want to print less than 1000 books for you because it costs less to print more if you got a book that you want to publish. In other words, the more you order, the less it costs us for publishing and printing. Going self-publishing usually means that people may not be able to afford to publish a lot. So be prepared to pay a little bit more secular. Be willing to pay the price. Then consider self-distribution, not as vital if you self-publish. You got to self-distribute, distribution is the key to success in business, not product development distribution, no matter how good your product is. If you do not have a distribution system, you will still be poor. Can I put it that way? A warehouse full of products is costing you money, so don't just publish because you want a book with your name on it, and then you keep it in the house, and then you try to peddle it to your friends. This is crazy because once all your ten friends got it, you still got 100 books. So, self-distribution has to be considered if you're going to self-publish. We have to think of it first when you want to self-publish; these are the pros you control the process. It's your book; it's your manuscript. You decide how the cover looks before you accept it. You choose how many to be printed, how many are distributed to you, what the cost is not always essential when you are self-publishing, you control the process, you control the cost, but you get to control distribution, you control the sales of your books yourself and those that control the price points of your material, you also control the promotion of it you've got to control the advertising and the marketing of it. This is a lot of work. So, when you're going to self-publish, get ready don't expect to compete with the top sellers. Now, if you were a public speaker and you travel a lot as some pastors, and you've got a market that you always deal with, then self-publishing may be a little bit easier for you because you have a captive market so that you can bring your products yourself to the market. You can advertise it to your market promoter to sell it to your market. You can even make deals with your market with discounts; self-publishing may show your market is big enough to pay what you pay to produce it. Publishing with a company, what are the pros? They got professional writers. This is something you pay for when you publish with a company you know, you may send a manuscript that is lousy to them, but they have writers who will take your manuscript, and when they finish with that you can compete with any book in any store they professional writers. So, a publishing company provides you with writers and editors. Also, they will produce a professional manuscript. They know how the industry-standard works so they can produce a manuscript that has the standard of international consumption. Some of the books that I see people write shouldn't even be in their own house. They sell it, but they're not up to standard. For example, the standard for industry-standard book is 168 pages write it down.

Also, professional designs. If a publishing company publishes your book, they got a department that deals with designing the book cover, designing the photographs, designing the fonts. They do all that work because they understand the industry-standard professional distribution system; publishing companies are already in the system; they know how to get your book to any bookstore. You know every time one of my new books come up four months before it's out, it's advertised. Sometimes, my books are being advertised, and I'm still writing the last chapters. That's how powerful their distribution system is. And they sell the book. To the wholesalers before I finish writing it, which puts pressure on the author. That's why you sign a contract. They sell the book before it's finished because it's in the system, and you can go online many times and see a book with my face on it. And the book isn't written yet because I'm in a publishing company where they have the distribution system so tight that they can sell it before it's produced, that's what they provide for you. They also provide professional promotion and advertising; that's what you pay for; they got industry catalogs, and industry retail distribution catalogs that you get your book goes in automatically before you even write it. And that catalog goes say to 30000 bookstores just like that. Those bookstores look at the books that are coming out. They say they order this. They have the system they promote. They also have what I call preset credibility publishing companies who are known in the market. The wholesalers know them. The retailers know them. The bookstore journals know them. So, when a company sends out say these five books are coming out in the fall, they send those to the wholesalers, and then, the retailers know that if a company called let's say Whittaker House publishing company sends you five books coming out they look at them because the company's name anybody but me. So, their credibility pre-sells your book if you go to a publishing company and that the whole sellers know much about then you may find that the movement of your matured book may be slow because the companies are not recognized by the industry yet be willing to pay the costs for publishing with a publisher. Publishers will charge you for publishing. You pay them for all of that. You know you pay them for all; you could even pay them for distribution if you want to. You can pay them for advertising in them that there are manuals and the journals you can pay for that, or you can say publish it. I want to promote it. I don't want you to advertise it. I'll do it myself. You can do that. You can choose from a menu which you want them to do, the only problem is remembering that you're not well-known in the distribution system, so you may want to pay that cost to get your name in the system, but you got to pay for that does it make sense because when you become known in the market, then they start paying you for your products. And when you become a bestselling author, they start negotiating with you. That's what you want to be. You want to be in a position eventually where you can say no and yes to different contracts because they know of your content, your quality, and your notoriety in the marketplace.

Be willing to submit to royalty standards. Now, you make your money in publishing royalties if you sell your books, of course, you make it through sales as well. But royalty is a residual income for a publishing company. If they were to accept your book to put in their system, they would say we would take on your book as one of our books. We put it in our system, and we give you 7 percent royalty on every book sold. And if your book sells well you know, the first print sells well, and they sold out. They say we go into second print and you can say look I want to renegotiate my royalty rate and if you become a bestselling author then the next book you negotiate with them, you can say I want 10 percent, in other words, your power to bargain for royalty depends on the success of your book, but there is a minimum you for royalty, I think is around 6 percent. Bestselling authors can get up to 50 percent, 30 percent depending on how big you are. I almost dead expect to be controlled by the publishers if they publish your work. This is important. You may decide. I want this cover design. They will tell you no, we're going to design this cover ourselves now. Don't fight them too much if you are an unknown author because they will design the cover based on the market demands. Some of you say my books are there, I know. Most of my books. They say you have an average of three seconds for them to pick your book up, three seconds; you do that also when you go to a bookstore, you take you and have three seconds to look at a book and decide to pick it up or not pick it up. So, the cover is important. So, when they talk about designing your cover, they will control that if you are unknown, they won't put your picture on the cover. But I want to pass them out to you. They don't know you said so, they may emphasize the title and put your picture away in the small back-room because you know you are unknown, so you don't fuss with them. If they are publishing your book, you are paying them to make you successful, so you have to give up some things to them publishing you; they may say look we can give you five percent royalty and as a passive model, so you get 30.

You know you pay for that. You got to plant a seed before you reap a harvest even in publishing. Well, let me cover with these principles of publishing but real quick cover design, promotion, distribution, marketing, and having a good foreword endorsement royalty. These are the basic words you need to be acquainted with when publishing. You have to have an understanding of graphics cover design promotion. How do you promote that product distribution? How do you get it to the market? Very important in marketing which audience you want your book to be marketed to. Now some of my books are marketed to business groups, so you'll find the designs and those books are very different. And then some of my books are sold to the Christian market, and some are sold to a family market, some marketed to men, some to women, so they design things based on the market and then you must be acquainted with things like endorsements. Well, that's what I could give you so far. Time has gone any questions. I'm sure there are a million of them.

Remember that I was just like you. I didn't know anything. I had to learn the industry; the industry is unique. So, jump into it and be successful. It's a strange industry.

About the Author

Bill Vincent is no stranger to understanding the power of God. Not only has he spent over twenty years as a Minister with a strong prophetic anointing, but he is now also an Apostle and Author with Revival Waves of Glory Ministries.

Bill offers a wide range of writings and teachings from deliverance to experiencing the presence of God and developing Apostolic cutting edge Church structure and drawing on the power of the Holy Spirit through years of experience in Revival and Spiritual Sensitivity. Now, Bill focuses mainly on pursuing the Presence of God and maintaining Revival.

RWG Publishing

I know there are many options, but RWG Publishing offers some of the best self-publishing options on the market. Check us out.

rwgpublishing@yahoo.com
https://rwgpublishing.com/

Recommended Books

By Bill Vincent
Overcoming Obstacles
Glory: Pursuing God's Presence
Defeating the Demonic Realm
Increasing Your Prophetic Gift
Increase Your Anointing
Keys to Receiving Your Miracle
The Supernatural Realm
Waves of Revival
Increase of Revelation and Restoration
The Resurrection Power of God
Discerning Your Call of God
Apostolic Breakthrough
Glory: Increasing God's Presence
Love is Waiting – Don't Let Love Pass You
By
The Healing Power of God
Glory: Expanding God's Presence
Receiving Personal Prophecy
Signs and Wonders

Signs and Wonders Revelations
Children Stories
The Rapture
The Secret Place of God's Power
Building a Prototype Church
The breakthrough of Spiritual Strongholds
Glory: Revival Presence of God
Overcoming the Power of Lust
Glory: Kingdom Presence of God
Transitioning to the Prototype Church
The Stronghold of Jezebel
Healing After Divorce
A Closer Relationship With God
Cover Up and Save Yourself
Desperate for God's Presence
The War for Spiritual Battles
Spiritual Leadership
Global Warning
Millions of Churches
Destroying the Jezebel Spirit
Awakening of Miracles
Deception and Consequences Revealed
Are You a Follower of Christ
Don't Let the Enemy Steal from You!
A Godly Shaking
The Unsearchable Riches of Christ

Heaven's Court System
Satan's Open Doors
Armed for Battle
The Wrestler
Spiritual Warfare: Complete Collection
Growing In the Prophetic
Faith
The Angry Fighter's Story
Understanding Heaven's Court System
Restoration of the Soul
Spiritual Warfare Made Simple
Aligning With God's Promises
Deep Hunger
Beginning the Courts of Heaven
Breaking Curses

Web Site:
www.revivalwavesofgloryministries.com

9 782488 686853